Cute Sweet Coloring Book

This Cake Coloring book belongs to:

_____

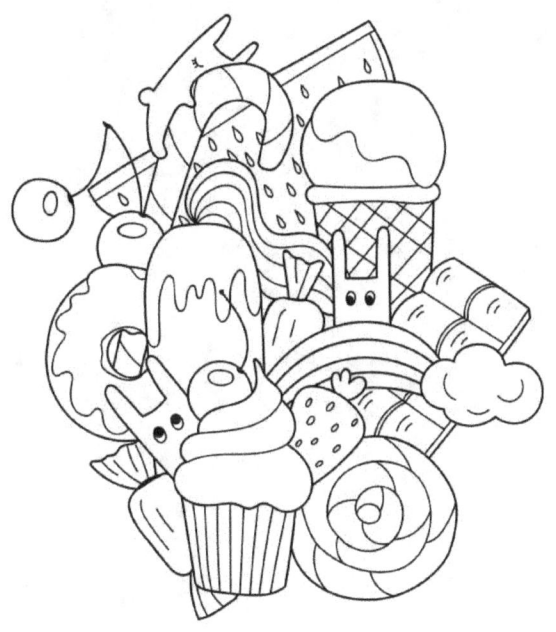

Copyright © 2019 Adult Coloring Books

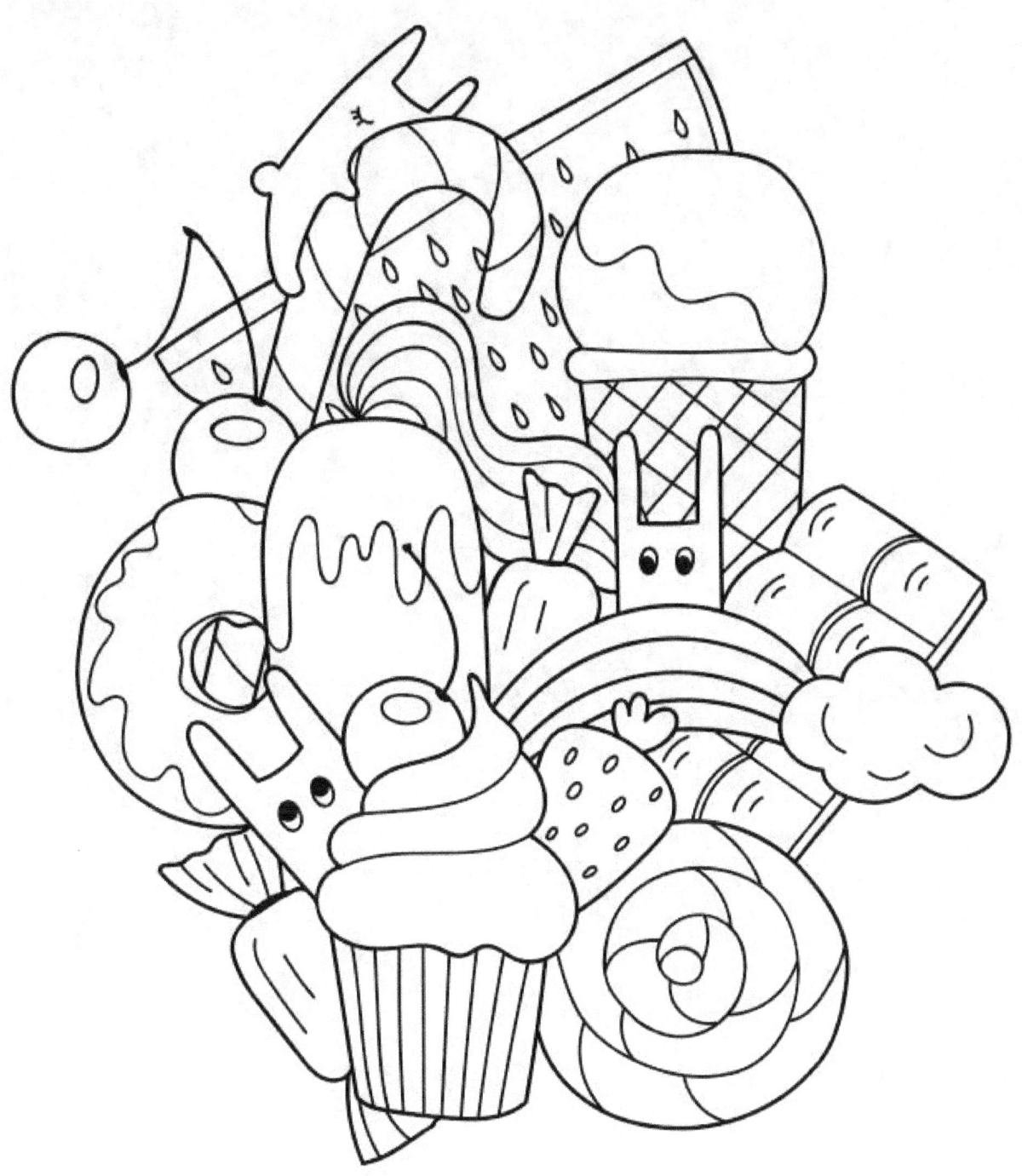

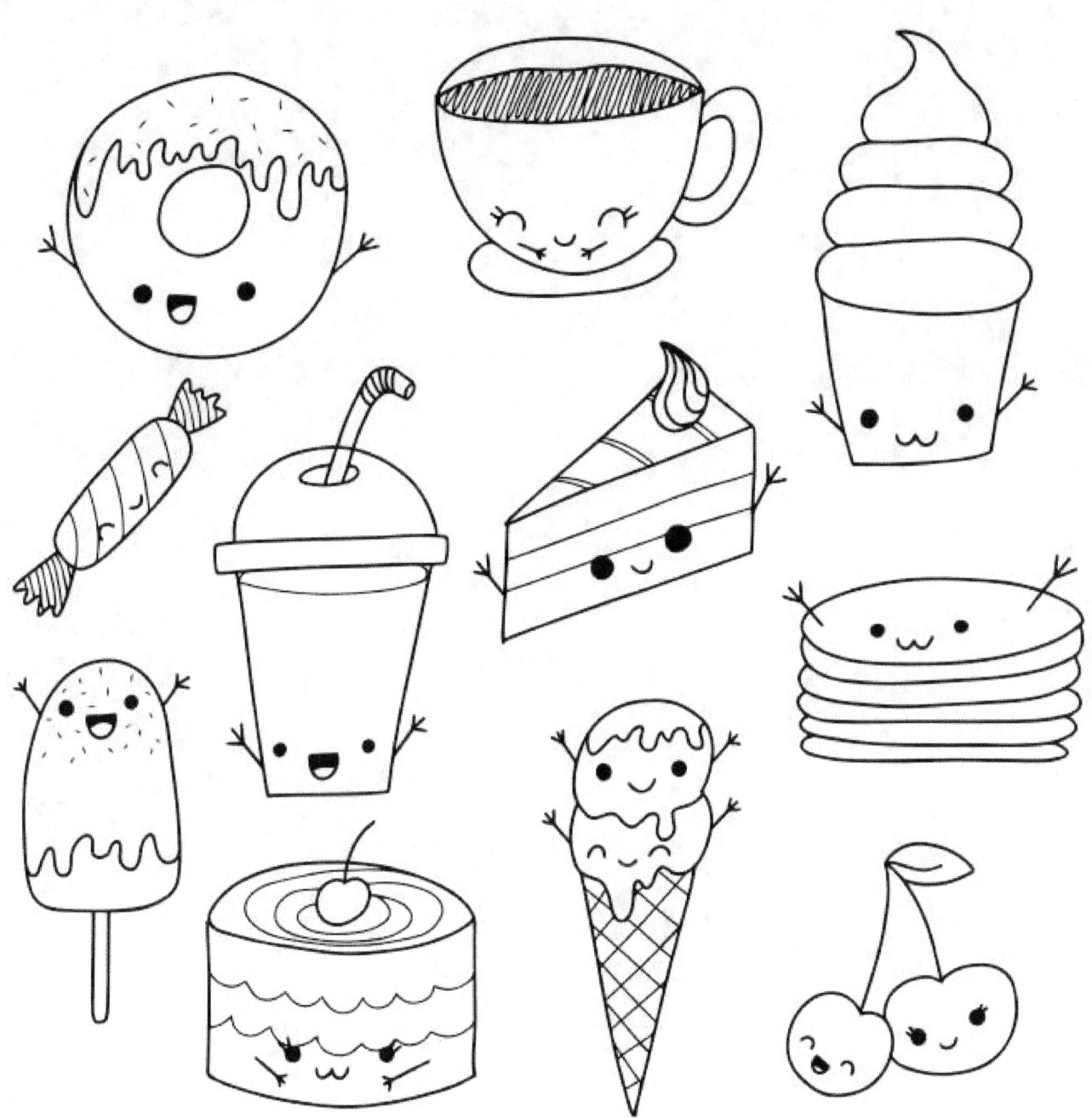

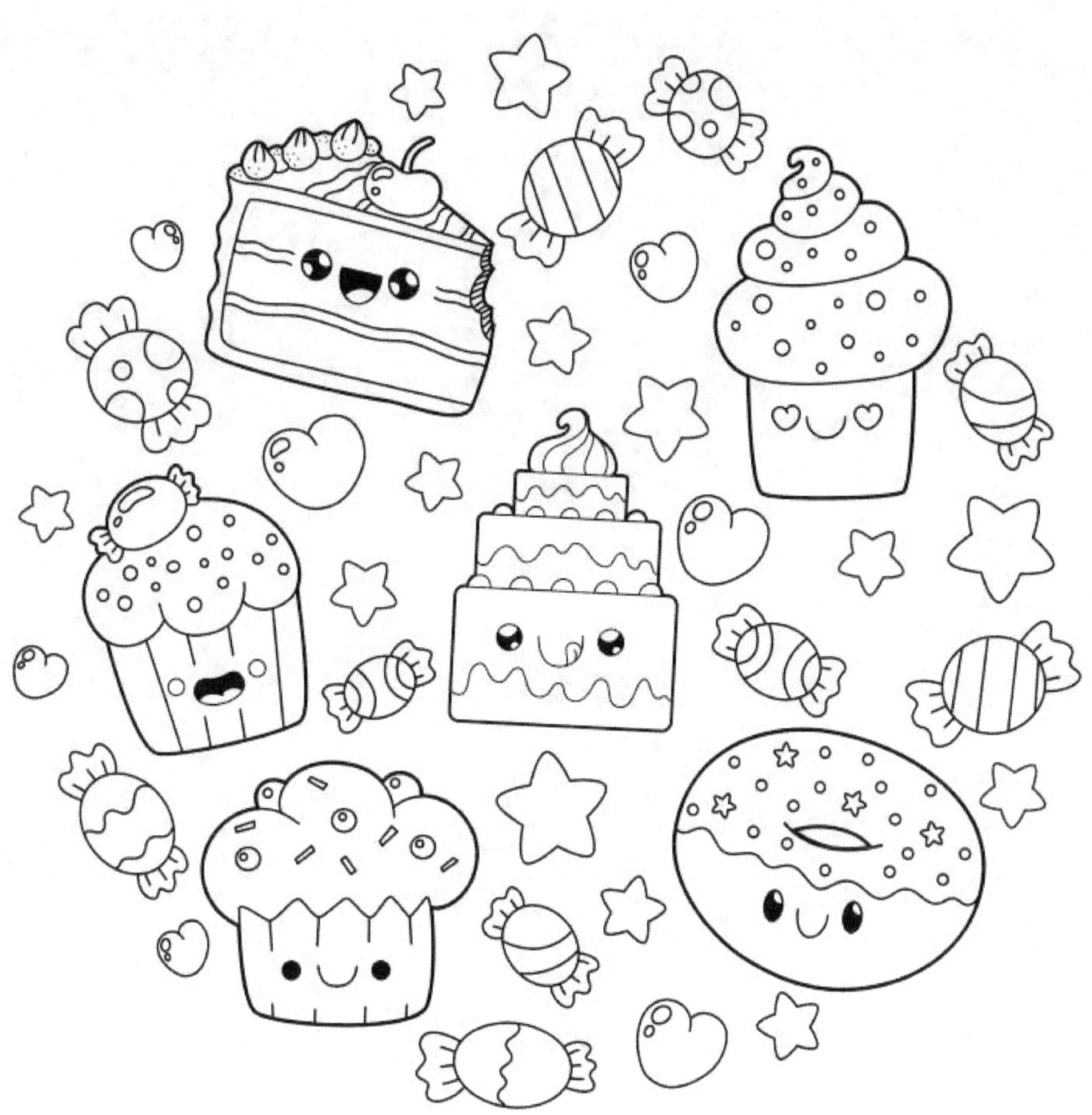

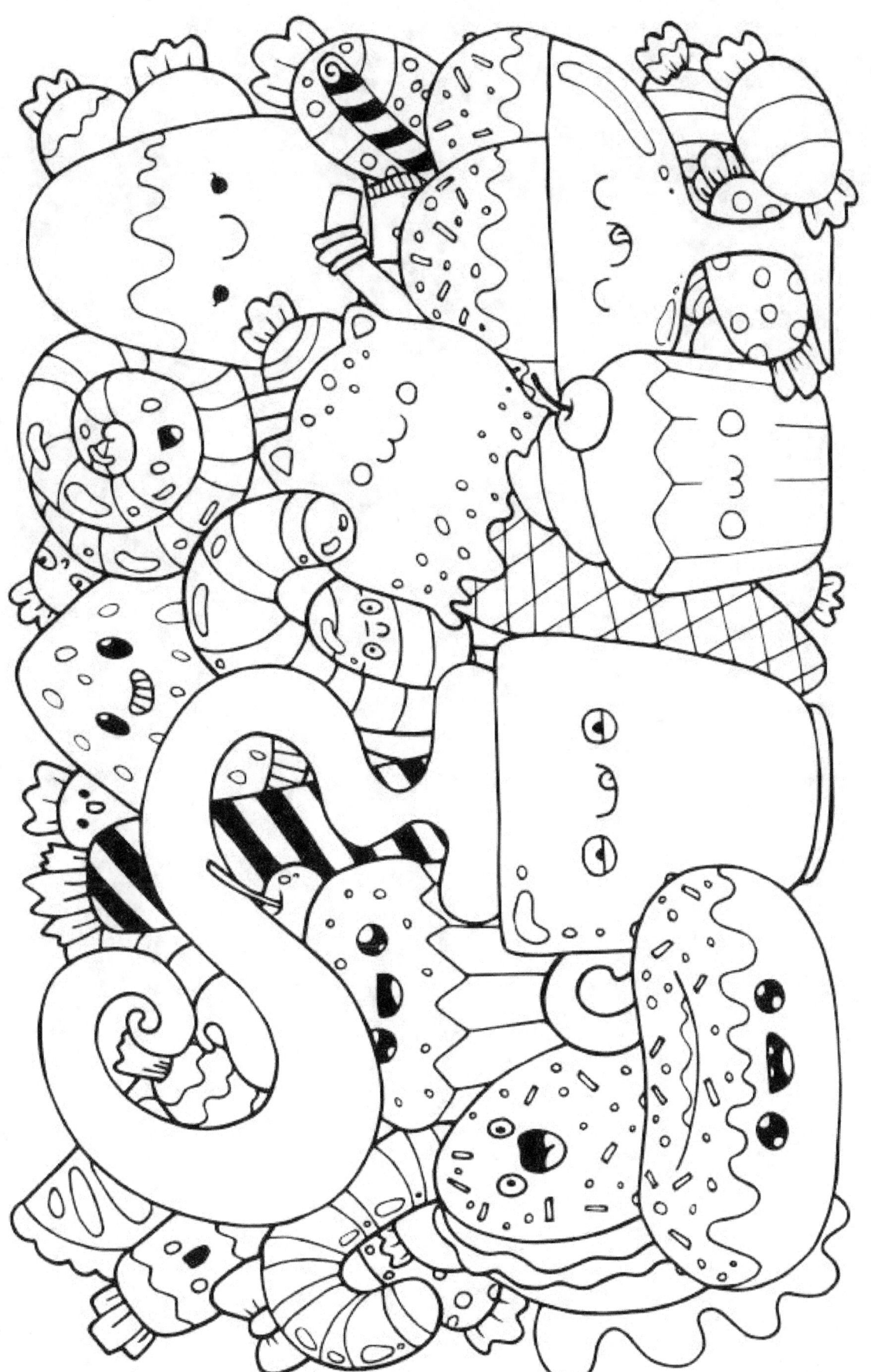

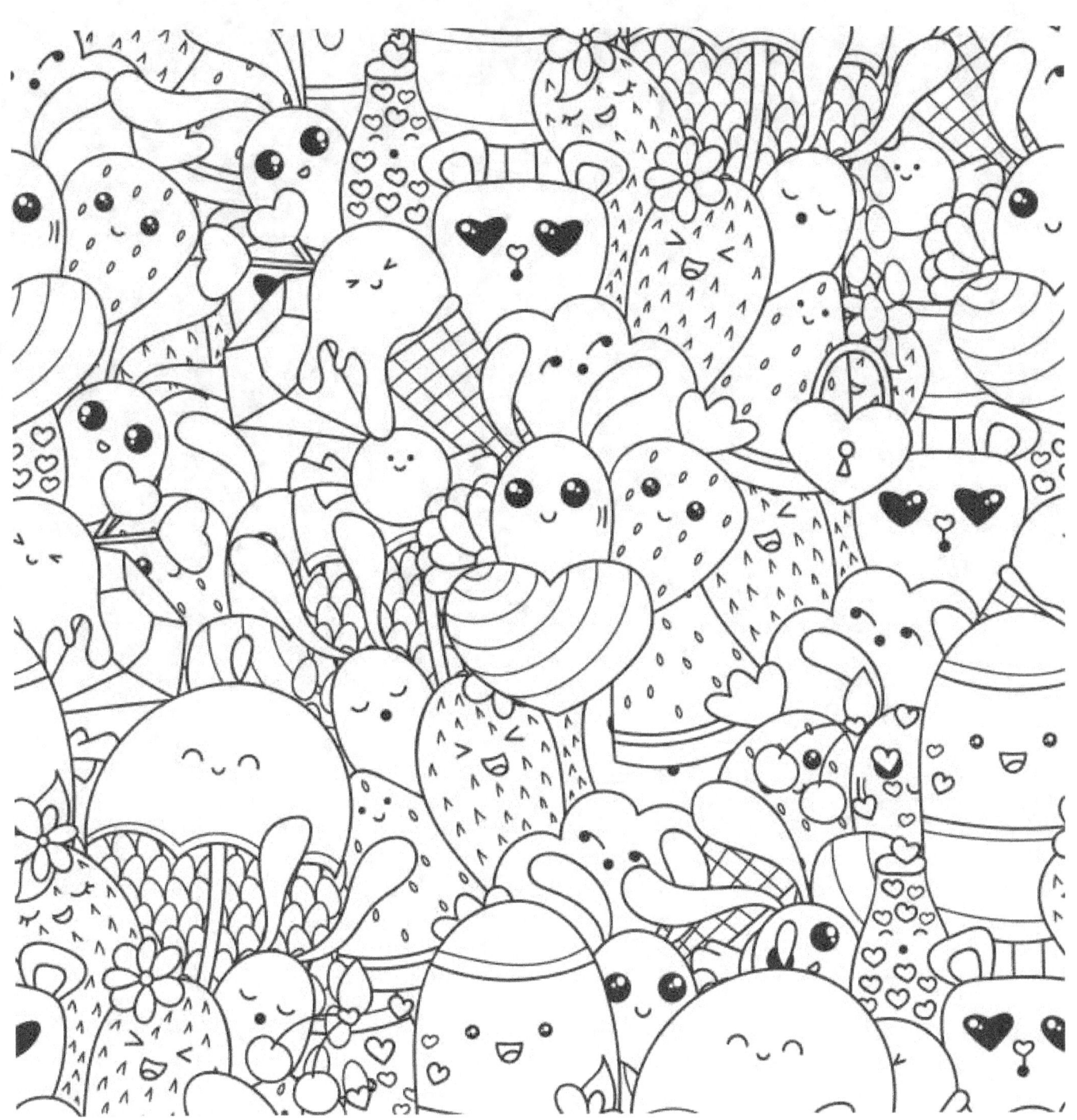

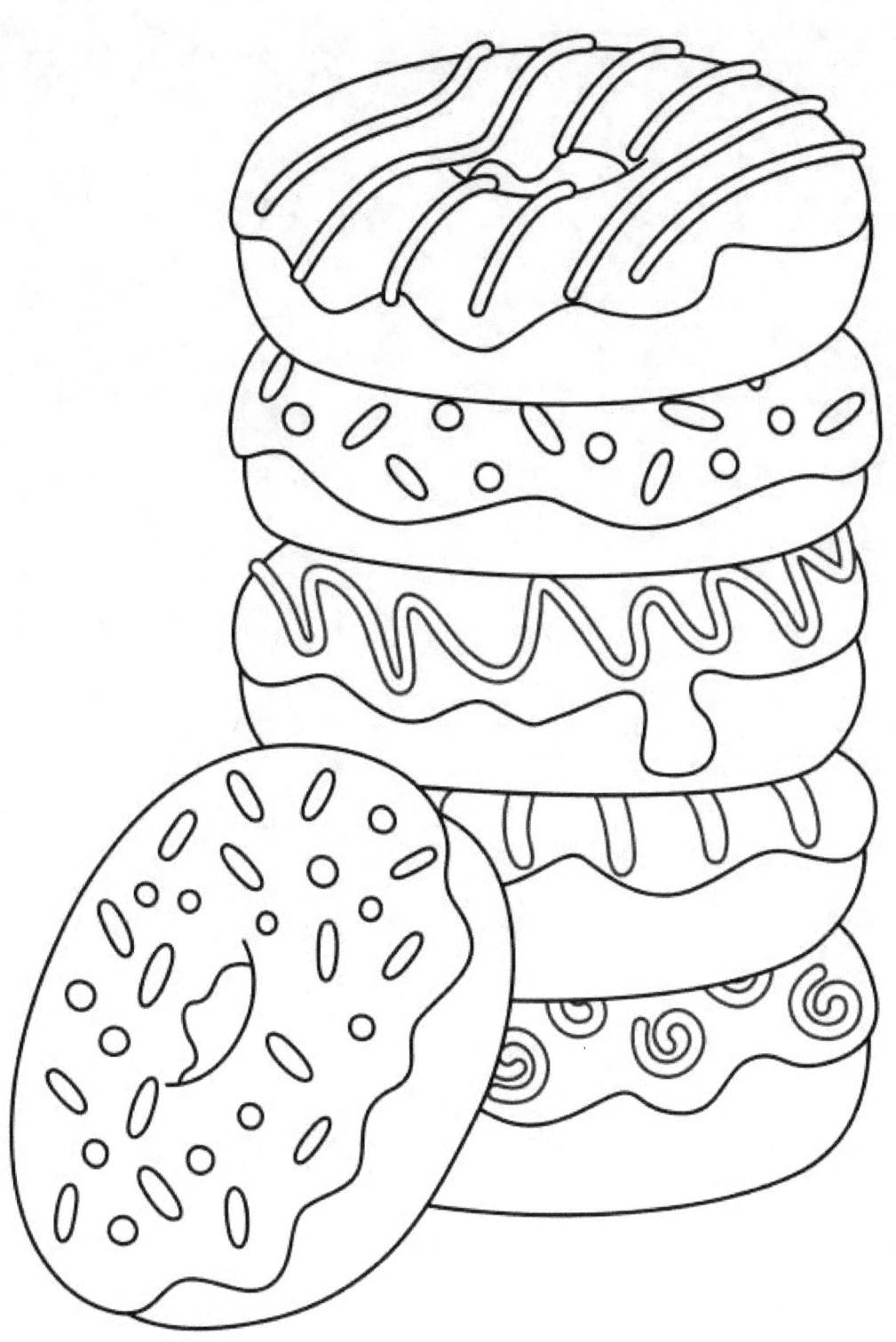

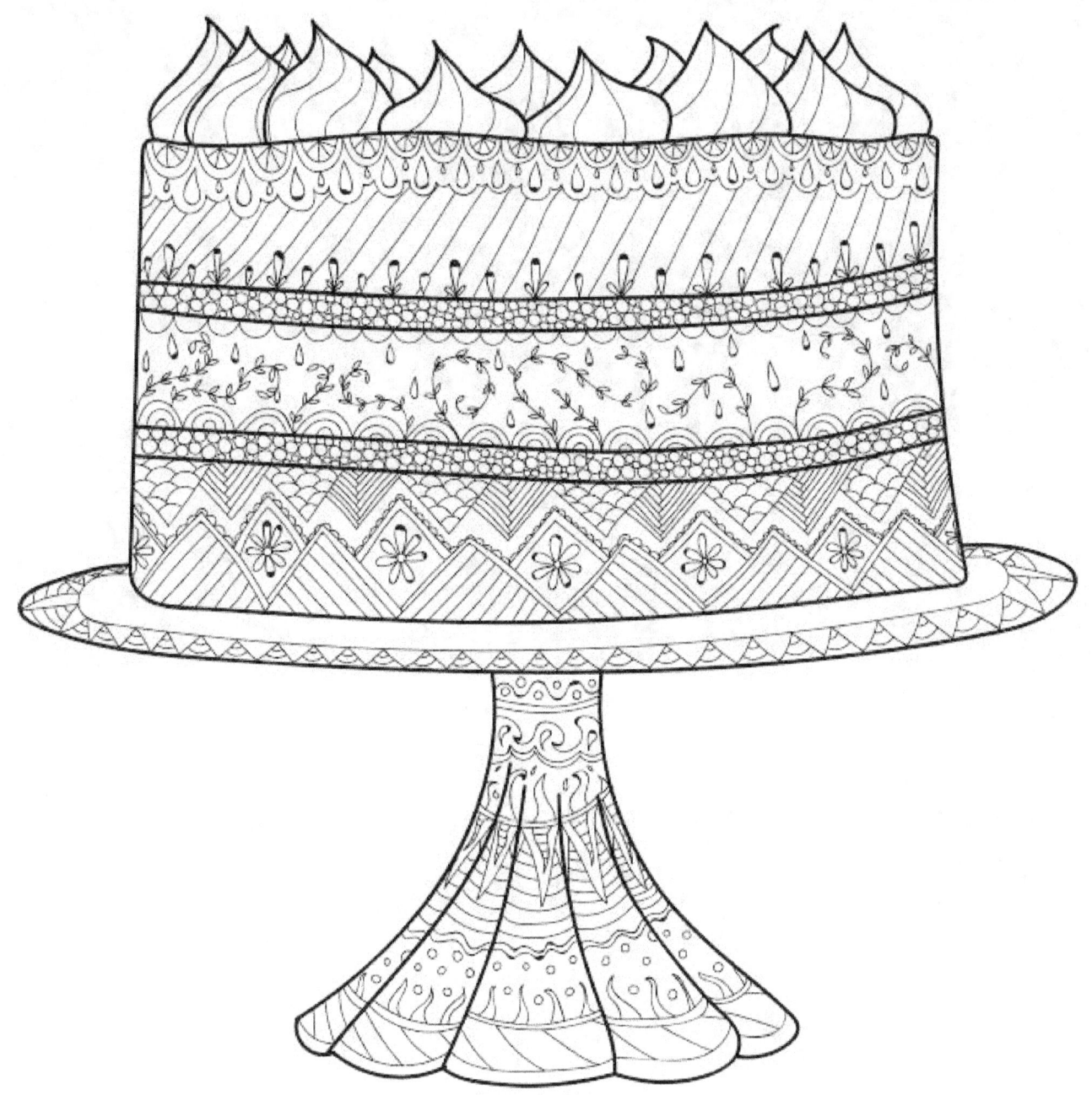

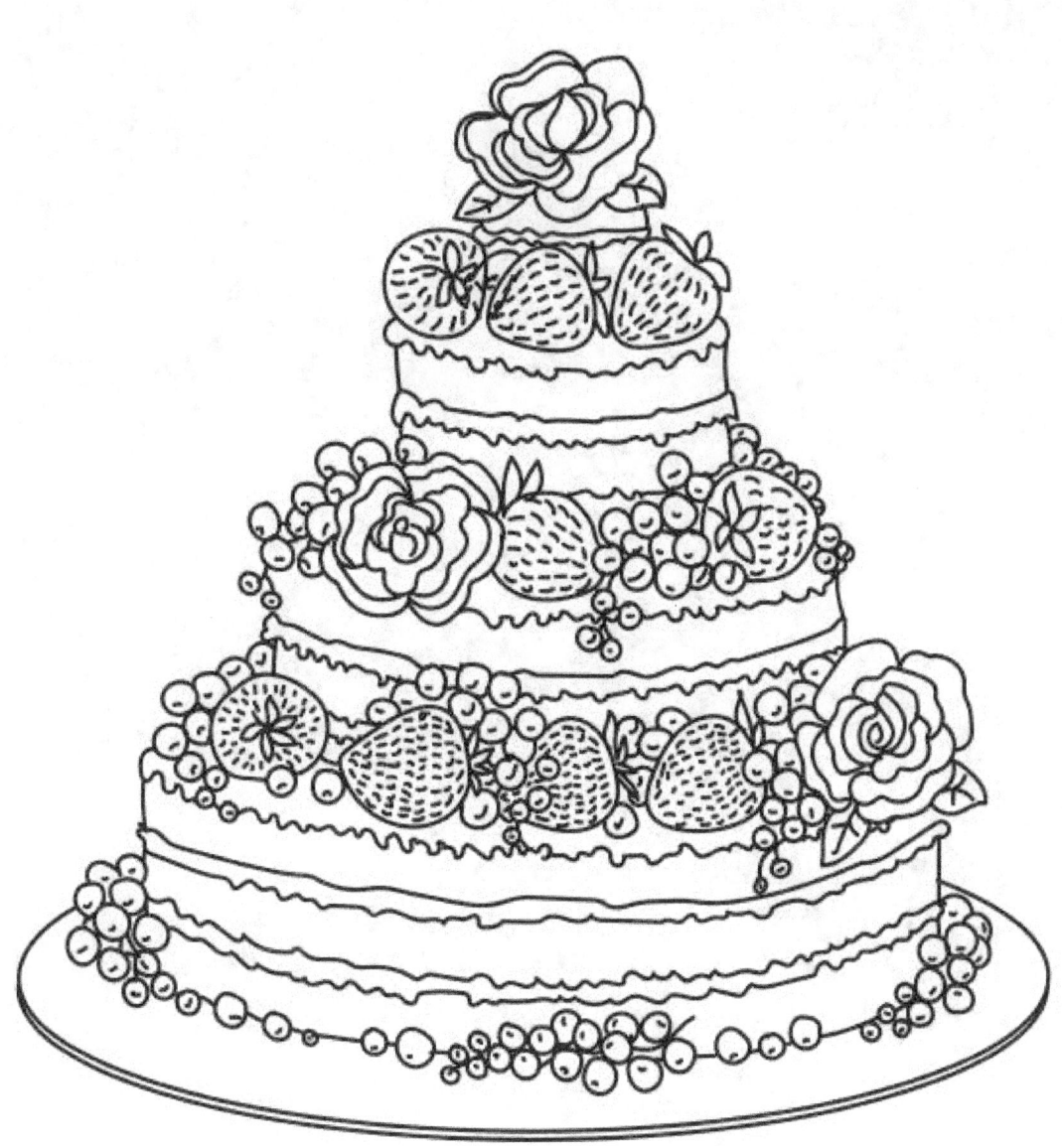

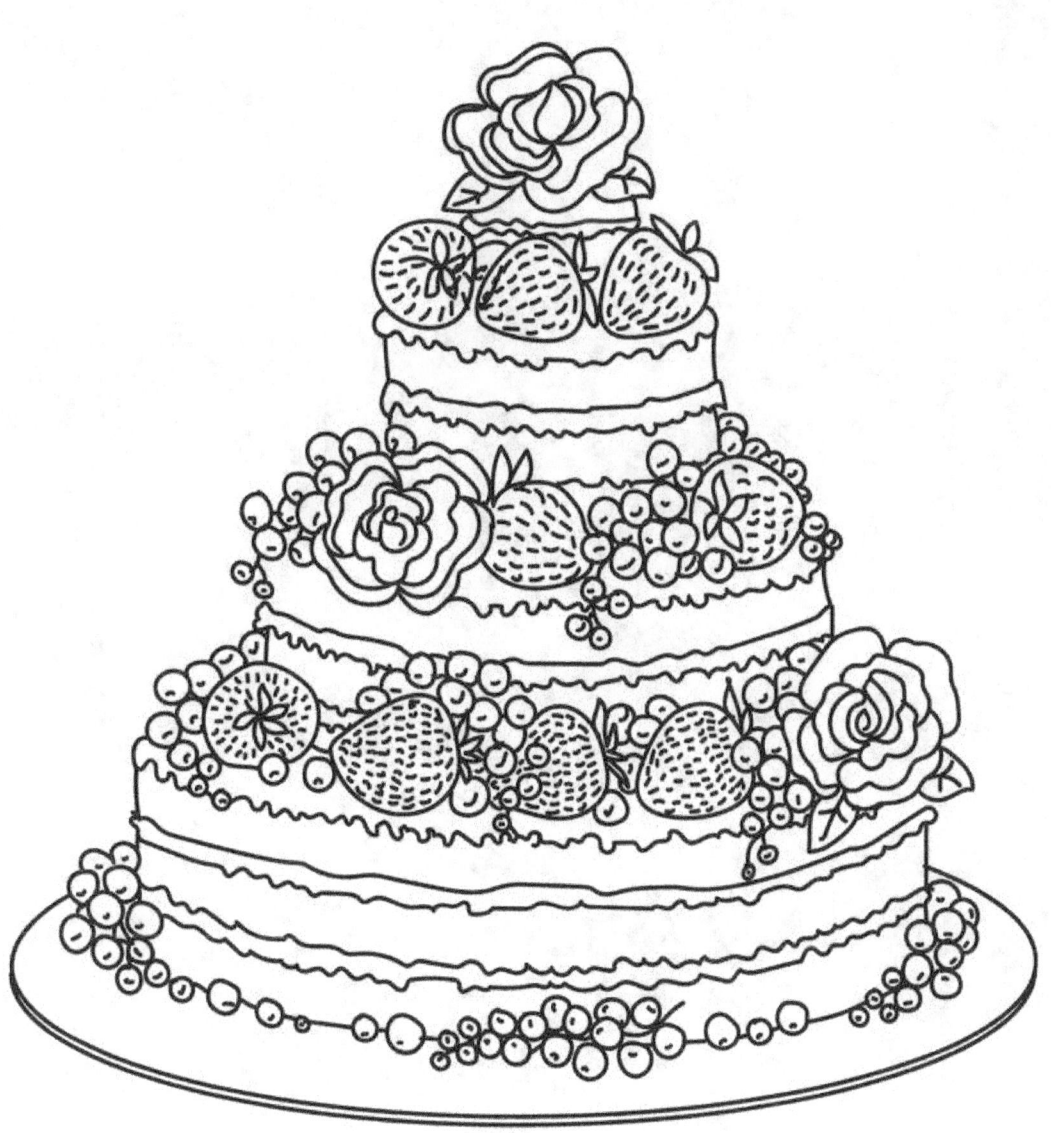

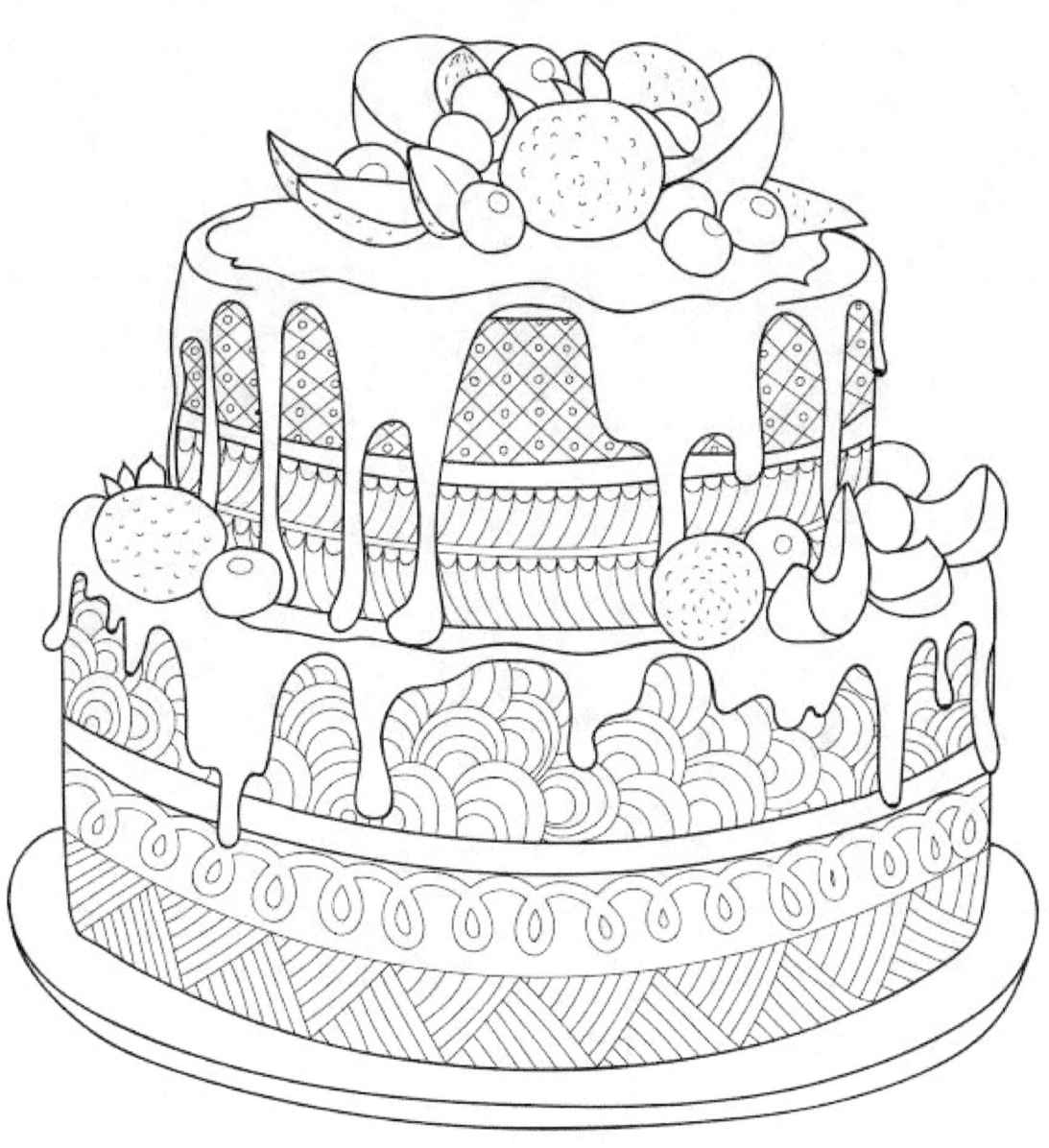

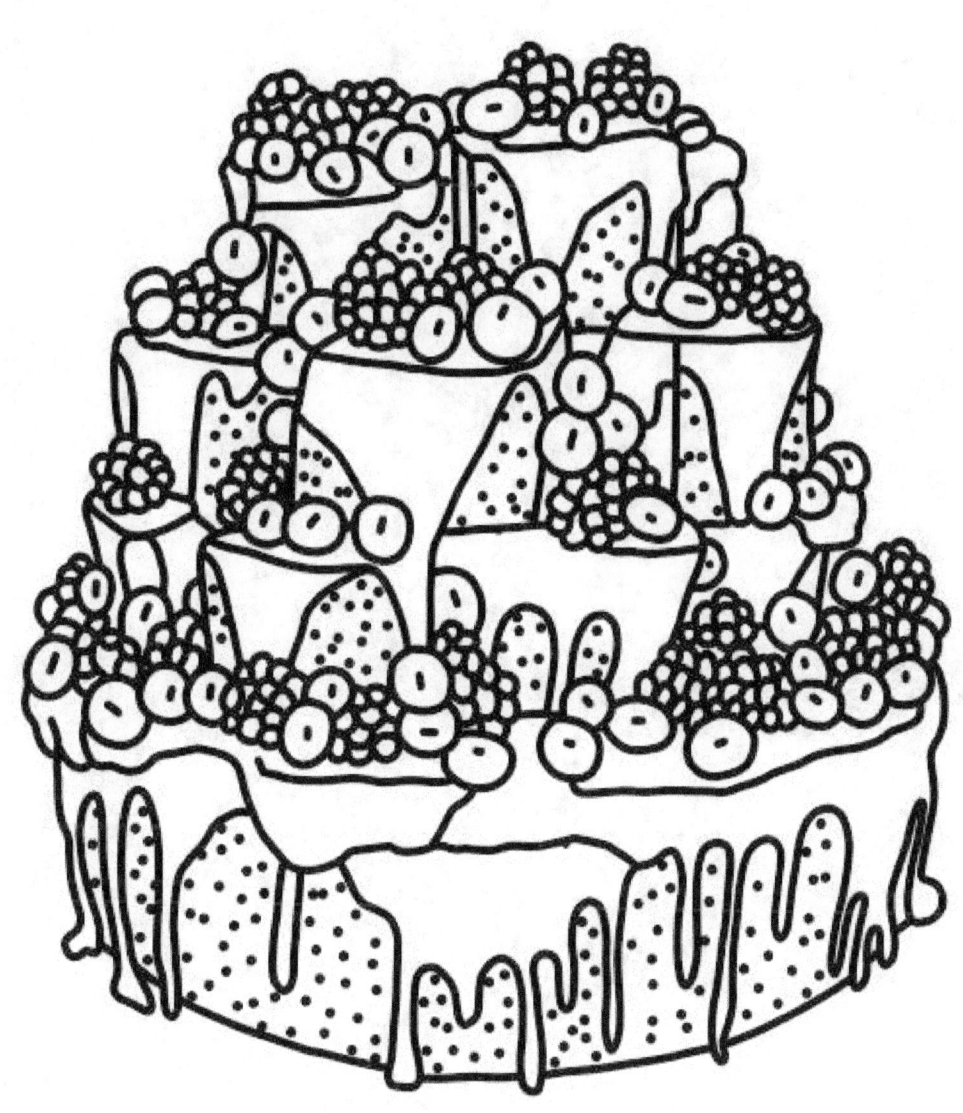

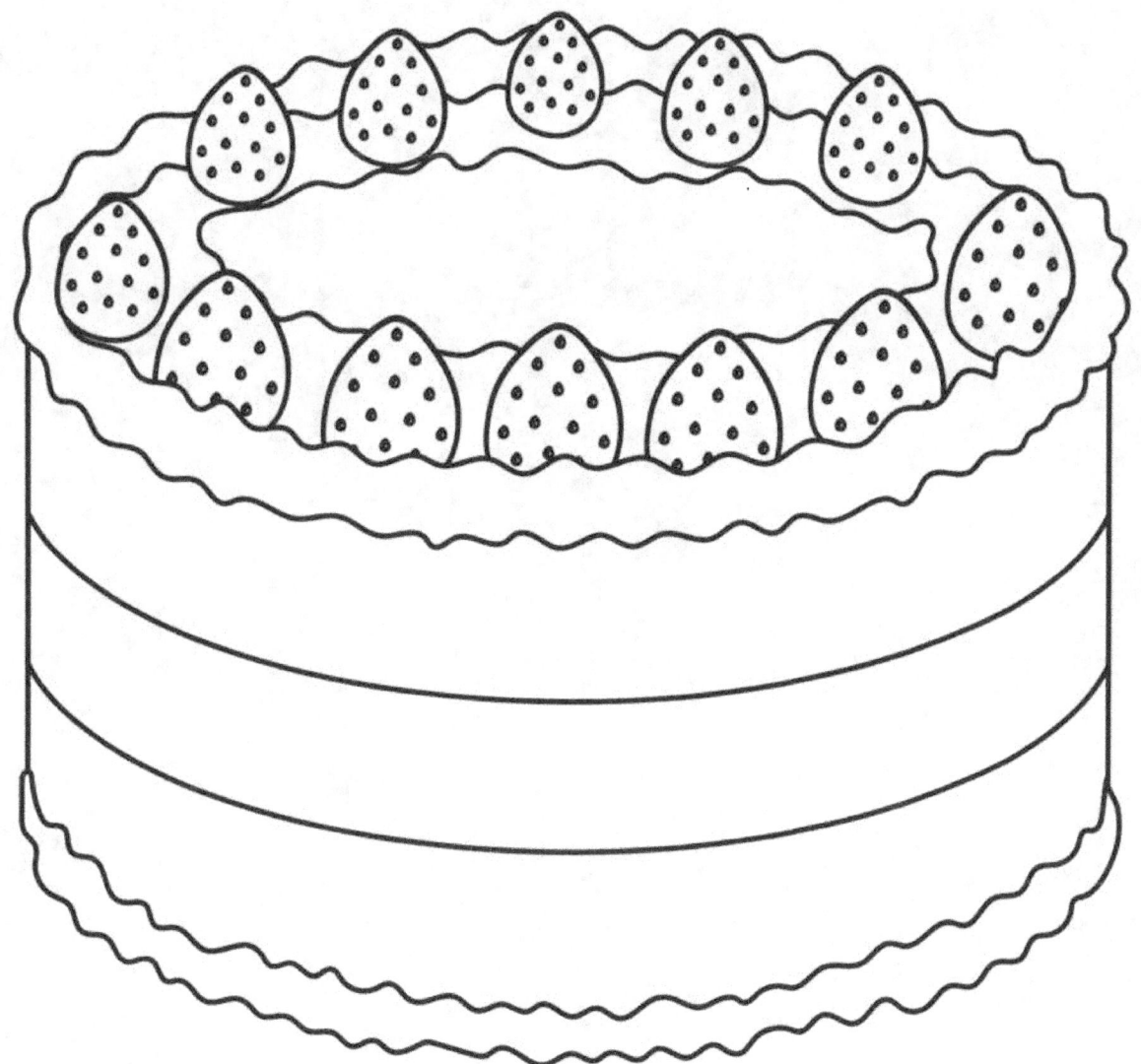

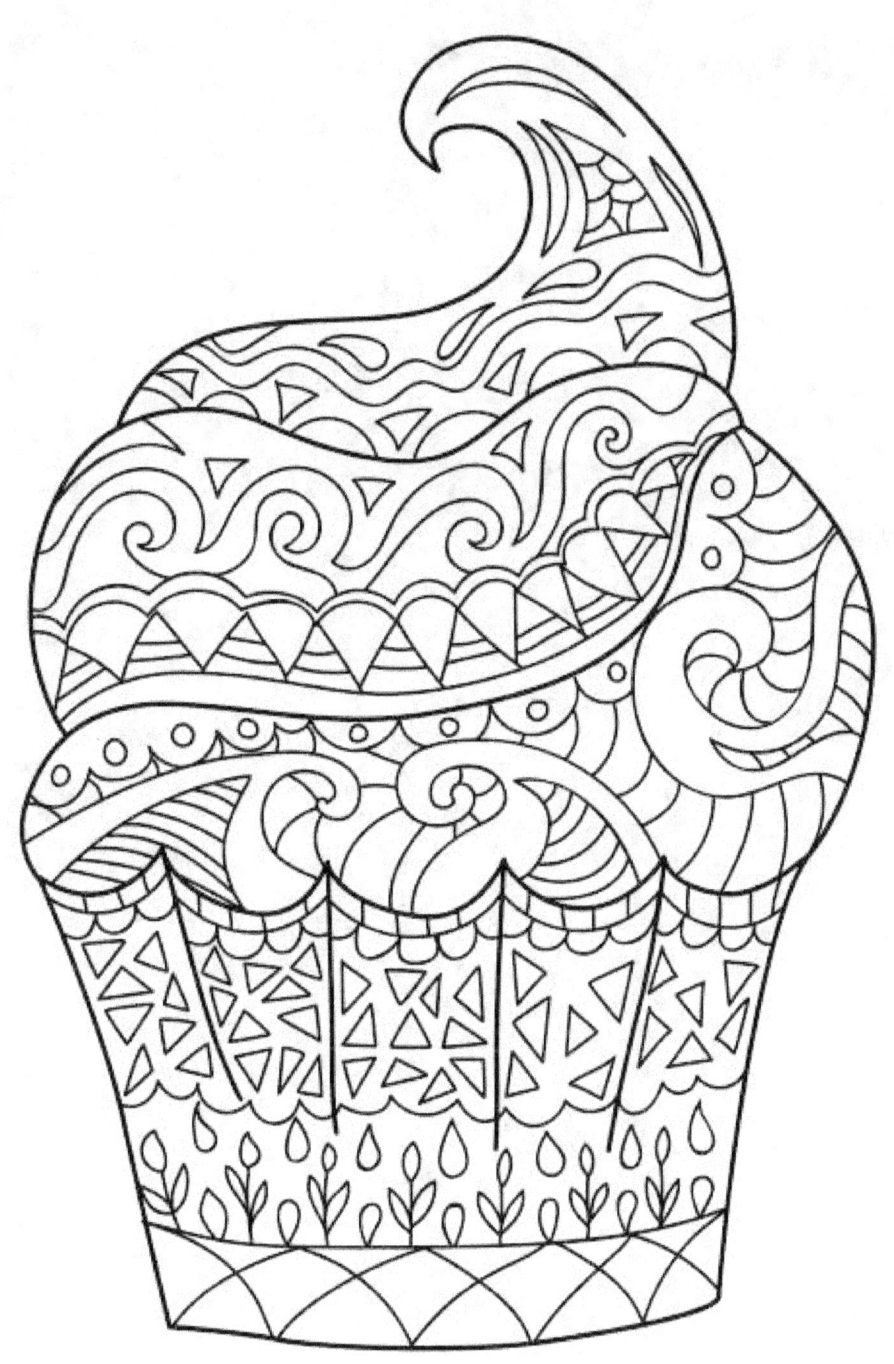

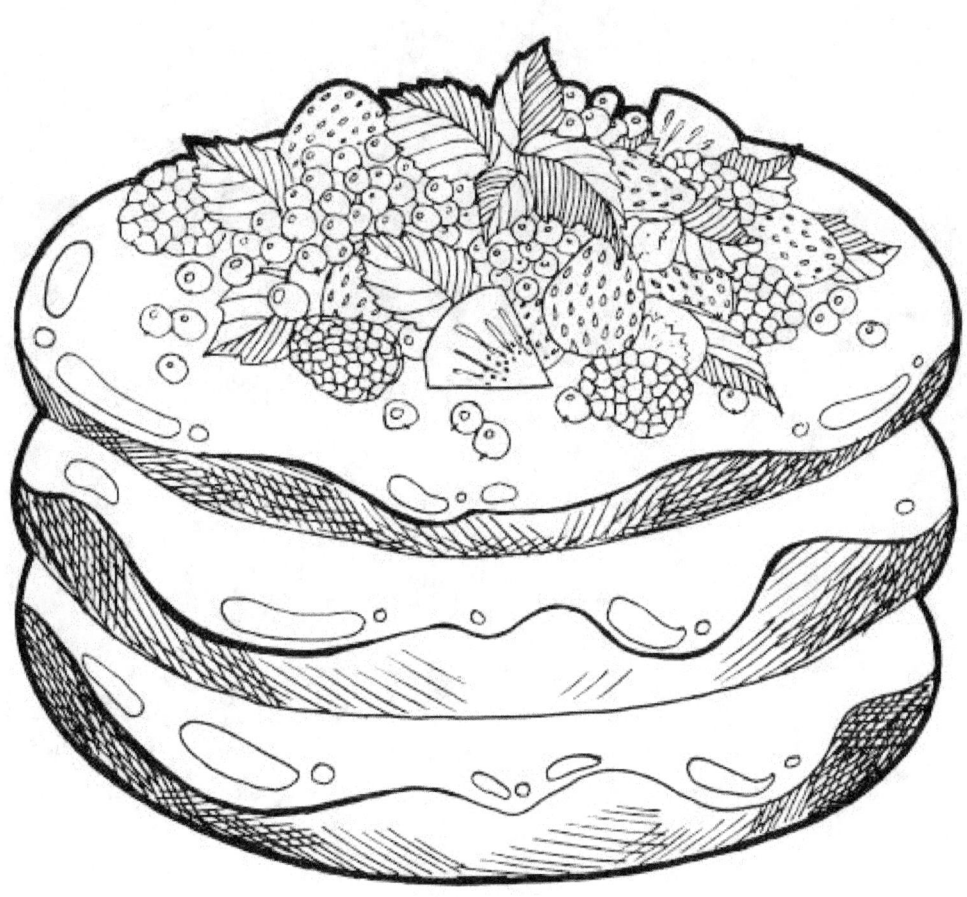

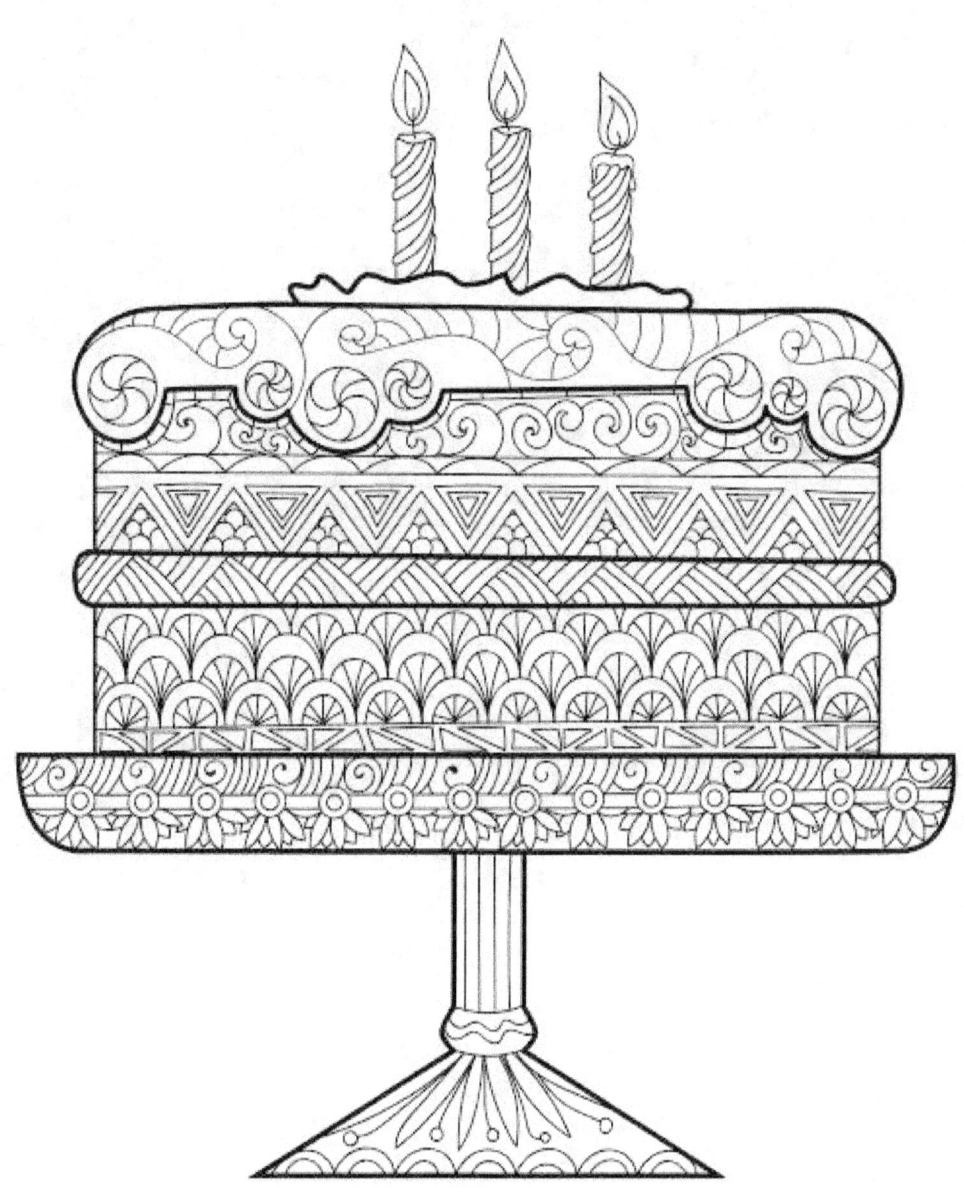

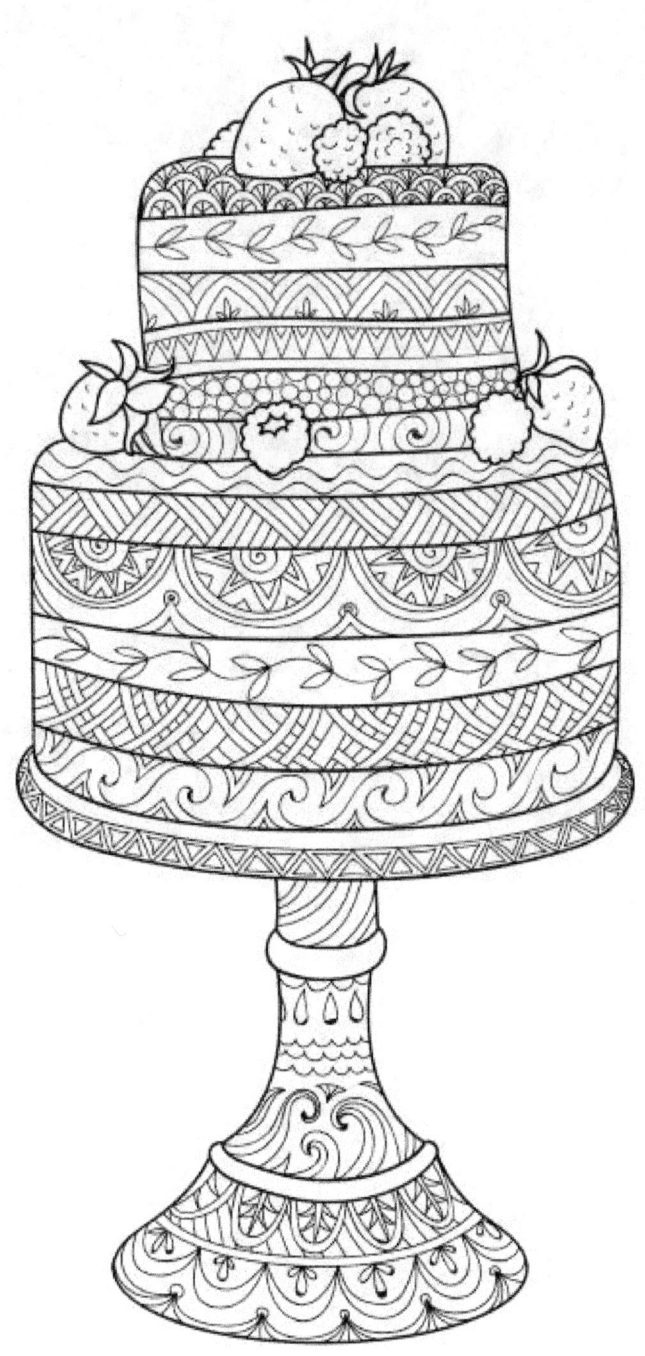

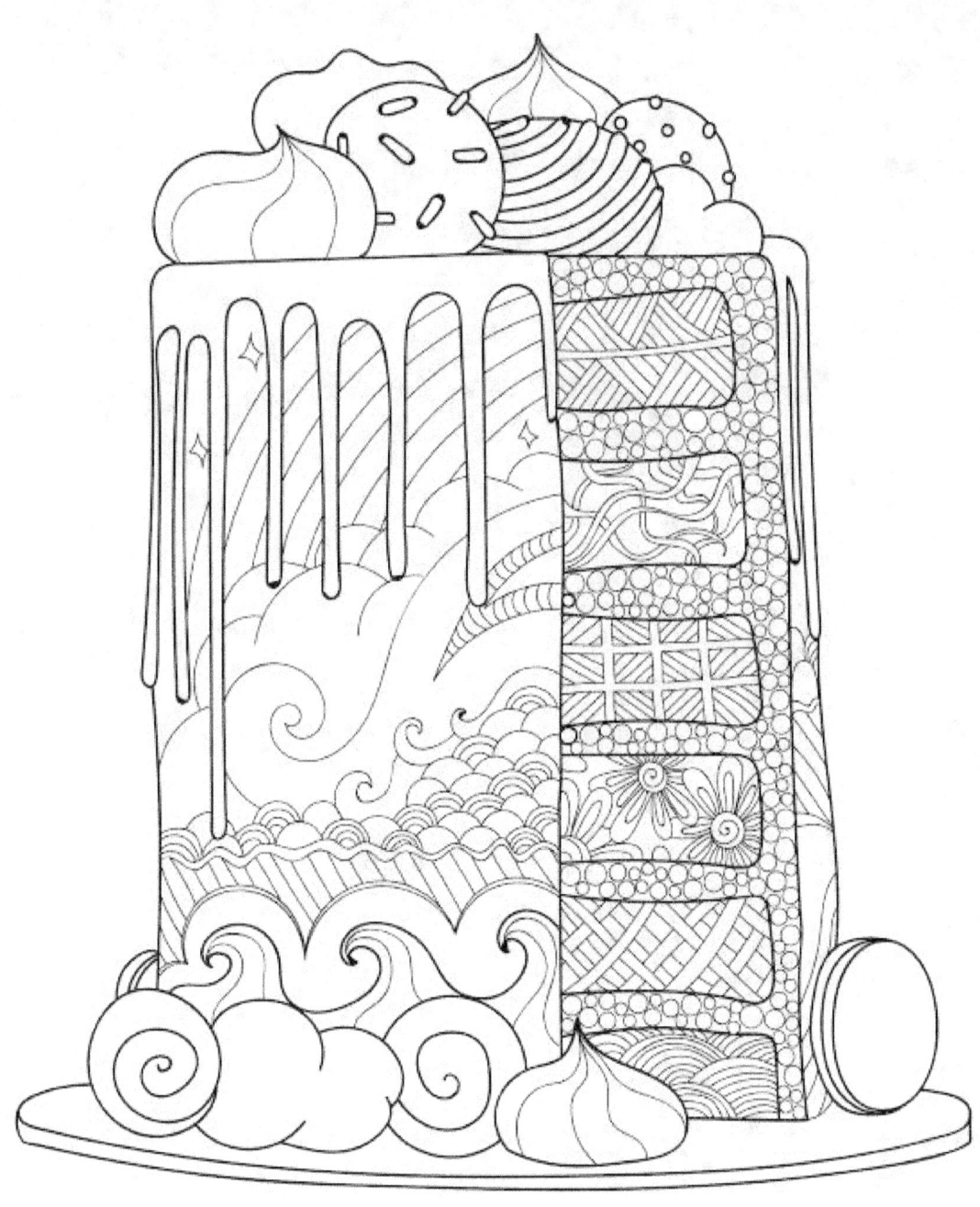

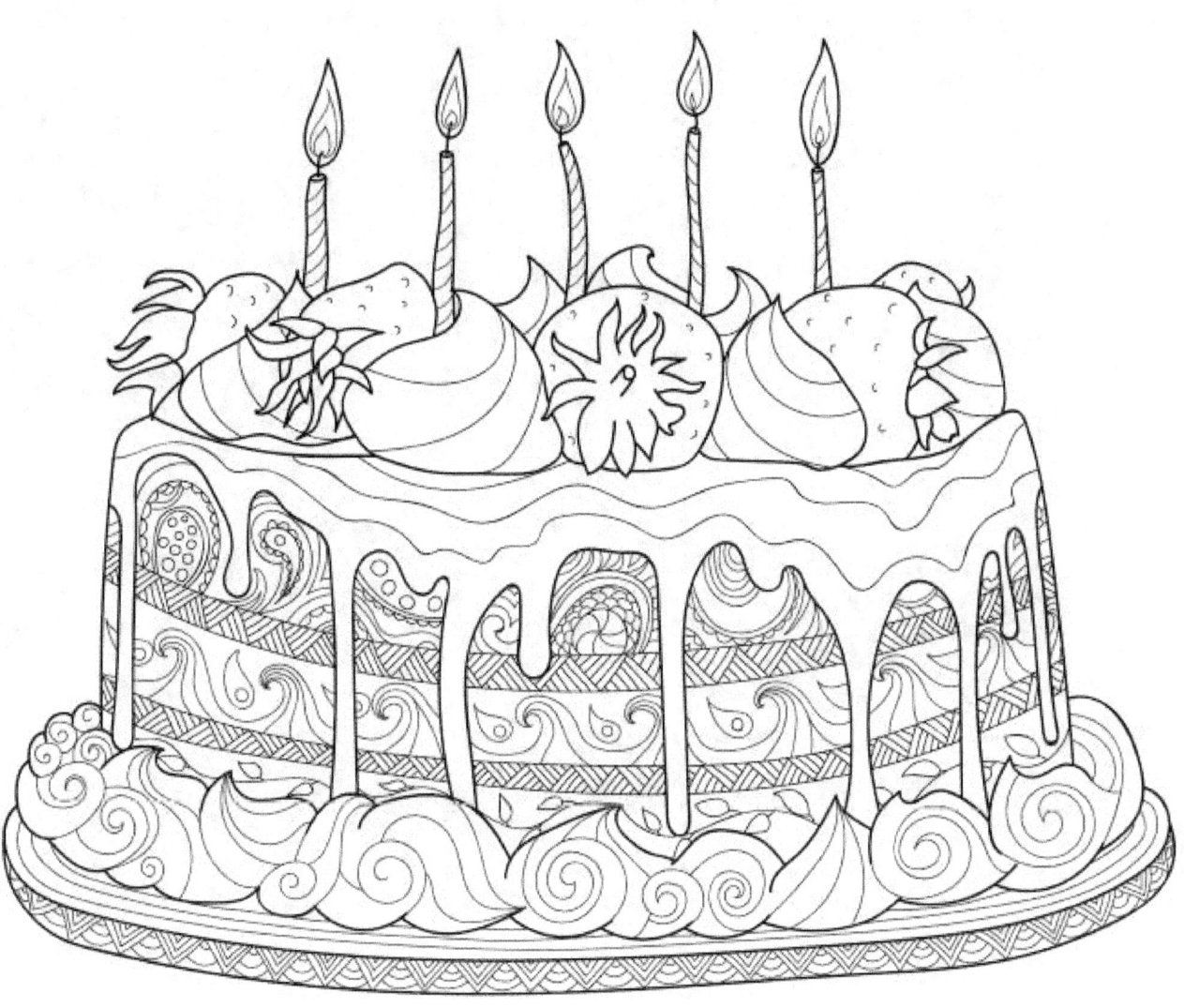

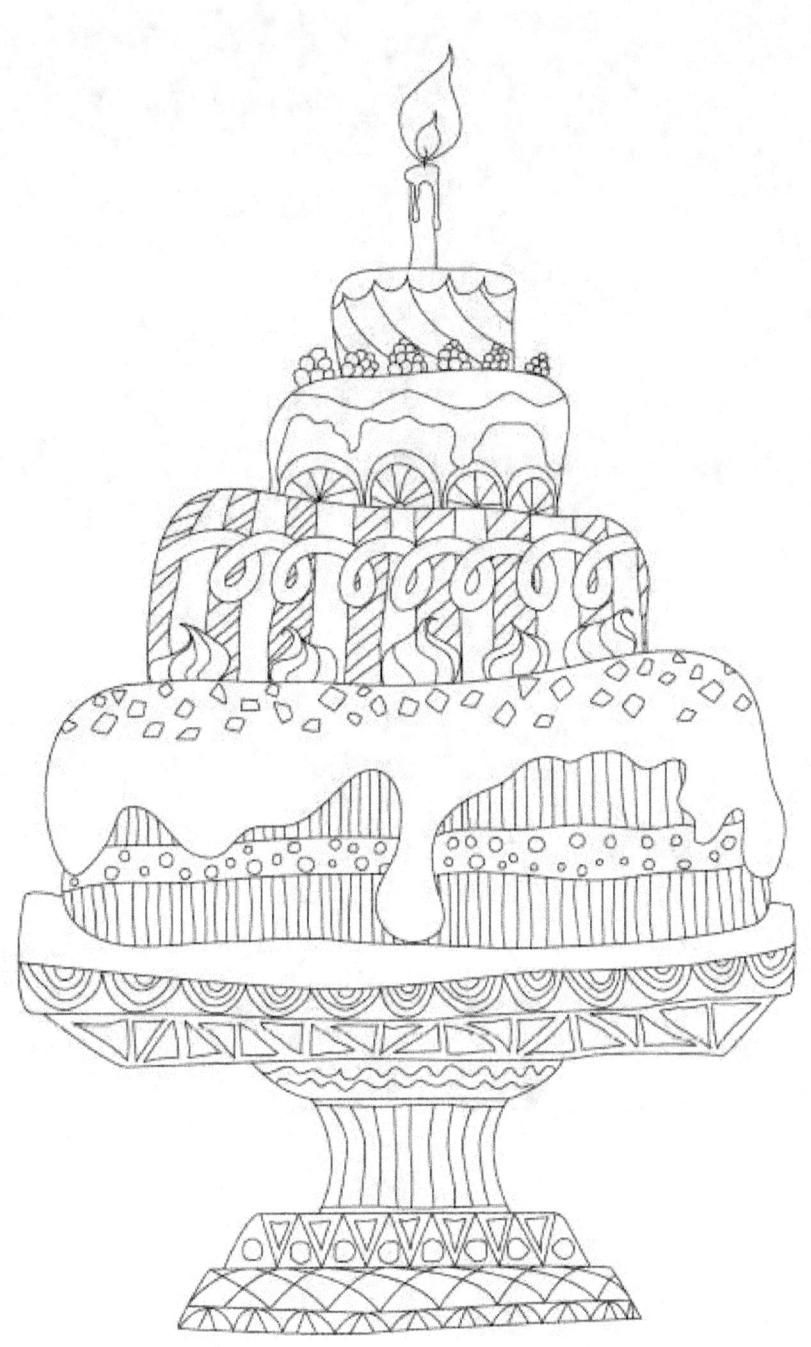

www.ingramcontent.com/pod-product-compliance
Lightning Source LLC
Chambersburg PA
CBHW081623220526
45468CB00010B/3002